P9-DJL-329

Tom Peters' Compact Guide to Excellence

Tom Peters and Nancye Green
Inspired by *Excellence Now: Extreme Humanism*

ISBN: 978-1-64687-124-7
MSRP: $22.50
Copyright ©2022 by Tom Peters.

IDEAPRESS
PUBLISHING

Published in the United States by Ideapress Publishing.
Ideapress Publishing | www.ideapresspublishing.com
All trademarks are the property of their respective companies.

Epigraph

"I want to work for a company that contributes to and is part of the community.

I want something not just to invest in; I want something to believe in."

Dame Anita Roddick

Introduction

In 1970, economist Milton Friedman outright dismissed the idea that businesses have any social or community responsibility—maximizing shareholder value was/is the alpha and omega of the existence of an enterprise. At the time, 50 percent of profits went to dividends, share buybacks, and such; and 50 percent went to workers, R&D, and other capital investments. By 2012, 42 years later, 91 percent of profits effectively went to shareholders, and 9 percent was left for employees, R&D, and the like. That is no less than staggering—and, among other things, a central driver of increasing inequity and social discord associated therewith.

In 1977, the managing director of McKinsey & Company, Ron Daniel, distressed by the failure of clients to execute the firm's brilliant strategies, commissioned a study that aimed to discover the organizational and leadership secrets of top performing companies. I was chosen to lead the team, and the result five years later was *In Search of Excellence*. The best performers had not followed Friedman's orders. They invested like maniacs in their people and research; they left no stone unturned in providing sterling experiences to their customers—and they were stellar, upright community members in the locales where they resided and did business. And, Dr. Friedman, their long-term financial results (and accompanying job creation record) topped the charts by a country mile.

My book, written with the late Bob Waterman, appeared in 1982, followed by 19 others—and I haven't changed my tune in the following 40 years. People first. Customer delight. An obsession with execution. The message has, however, been enriched. Now I rant and rave about more-more-more women in top slots—for reasons of business excellence, not "affirmative action." I champion product and service design that without exception betters our lives, warms our hearts, and cools our planet. I insist upon a "mind-blowing" commitment to training—Capital Investment #1. Comprehending and acting upon the fact that all good things come from a peerless population of inspired frontline managers—Corporate Asset #1. I reach way beyond the confines of money-grubbing Fortune 500 boardrooms and tout the achievements of our many, many stellar SMEs (Small- and Medium-sized Enterprises) as innovators and job creators. And, above all, I emphasize the existential necessity for a business and businesses collectively to model moral behavior and to go to extreme lengths to support the communities in which their employees live and in which they do business.

In this short treatise, which I label *Tom Peters' Compact Guide to Excellence*, I call upon others to tell my story. Others who have been down in the trenches and created extraordinary places to work in which their teams have thrilled customers and made great contributions to their communities. This treatise is, indeed, short; it is the essence of the essence of my work as expressed by our most prized enterprises and their leaders. I hope it resonates with you. And, more important, I hope it leads to commitment and actions around these very humane (and, indirectly, profitable) ideas.

The material is largely extracted from my latest book, *Excellence Now: Extreme Humanism*. As we come to terms with the recent debilitating and horrifying pandemic, confront extreme wealth inequality, and wrestle with destabilizing technological revolutions still in their infancy, it is my conclusion that "Extreme Humanism"—putting people *really* first and helping them prepare for a rocky future, vigorously and passionately supporting our communities, providing products and services that stun our clientele with their excellence and verve, serving our ailing planet—is, perhaps counterintuitively, the best path forward. Moreover, it is a path that can engender purpose and pride in all of us who perform the work.

This "excellence/extreme humanism synopsis" is organized in terms of 13 themes.

Enjoy, absorb, act!

This
"compact guide"
is organized
around 13
central themes.

Execution:
The "Last
95 Percent"

Amateurs talk about strategy.

> " **Strategy is a commodity. Execution is an art.** "

Peter F. Drucker

> " **Amateurs talk about strategy. Professionals talk about logistics.** "

USMC General Robert Hilliard Barrow

" Execution is the job of the business leader. . . .

When assessing candidates, the first things I look for are energy and enthusiasm for execution. . . .

Does she talk about the thrill of getting things done, or does she keep wandering back to strategy or philosophy?

Does she detail the obstacles that she had to overcome?

Does she explain the roles played by the people assigned to her? "

Larry Bossidy, former CEO of Honeywell International, and Ram Charan, *Execution: The Discipline of Getting Things Done*

"For want of a nail, the shoe was lost,
For want of a shoe, the horse was lost,
For want of a horse, the rider was lost,
For want of a rider, the message was lost,
For want of a message, the battle was lost,
For want of a battle, the war was lost,
For want of a war, the kingdom fell,
And all for the want of a nail. "

Thirteenth-century proverb

" Don't forget execution, boys.
It's the all-important last 95%. "

McKinsey managing director, to one of my project teams

2

**Hard Is Soft.
Soft Is Hard.**

My life in six words . . . * **

Hard
(Numbers/Plans/Org Charts)
Is Soft.

Soft
(People/Relationships/Culture)
Is Hard.

Tom Peters

---

*Best guess is that I first used this phrase in an internal
McKinsey presentation in early 1978.
**My greatest aspiration is to break the chokehold that the
so-called "hard stuff" has on businesspersons, business lingo,
and MBA programs the world over.

Google's Big,
Soft Surprises

" Project Oxygen shocked everyone by concluding that, among the eight most important qualities of Google's top employees, STEM expertise comes in dead last. The seven top characteristics of success at Google are all soft skills: being a good coach; communicating and listening well; possessing insights into others (including others' different values and points of view); having empathy toward and being supportive of one's colleagues; being a good critical thinker and problem solver; and being able to make connections across complex ideas. Those traits sound more like what one gains as an English or theater major than as a programmer. . . . ▶

Project Aristotle . . . further supports the importance of soft skills even in high-tech environments. Project Aristotle analyzes data on inventive and productive teams. Google takes pride in its A-teams, assembled with top scientists, each with the most specialized knowledge and able to throw down one cutting-edge idea after another. Its data analysis revealed, however, that the company's most important and productive ideas come from B-teams comprised of employees who don't always have to be the smartest people in the room.

Project Aristotle shows that the best teams at Google exhibit a range of soft skills: equality, generosity, curiosity toward the ideas of your teammates, empathy, and emotional intelligence.

And topping the list: emotional safety. No bullying. **"**

Valerie Strauss, "The Surprising Thing Google Learned About Its Employees—and What It Means for Today's Students," *Washington Post*

Rich Karlgaard:
The Soft Edge

I like *Forbes* publisher Rich Karlgaard's hard-soft definition/distinction at least as much as my own.

" I believe the business world is at a crossroads, where hard-edge people are dominating the narrative and discussion. . . .

The battle for money and attention boiling inside most companies and among most managers is that between the hard and soft edges. . . . ▶

Far too many companies invest too little time and money in their soft-edge excellence. . . .

This mistake has three
main reasons:

The hard edge is easier
to quantify. . . .

Successful hard-edge investment
provides a faster return on
investment. . . .

CEOs, CFOs, COOs, boards of
directors, and shareholders speak
the language of finance. . . . ▶

Here's the case for investing time and money in your company's soft edge:

Soft-edge strength leads to greater brand recognition [and] higher profit margins. . . . [It] is the ticket out of Commodityville.

Companies strong in the soft edge can often survive a big strategic mistake or cataclysmic disruption. . . .

Hard-edge strength provides a fleeting advantage . . . necessary to compete, but not sufficient to win. "

Rich Karlgaard, *The Soft Edge: Where Great Companies Find Lasting Success*

Community/
Purpose

Community

A business *is* a community.

Collectively, businesses *are* the community.

Business has a primary obligation to the growth of every employee, to the diversity of its workforce, to the well-being and prosperity of the communities in which it does business, the communities in which its employees live, and to the planet.

Business, as a community and a community within communities, has the obligation to behave in a visibly moral fashion.

Business as a community and a contributor to communities has an obligation to create products and services which inspire—and which aim to make the world a bit better.

" There is no business excellence without community excellence. Think deeply about this. "

Tom Peters

"The Business of Business Should Not Be Just About Money.

It Should Be About Responsibility."

The late Dame Anita Roddick created and led an enterprise, The Body Shop, now with 3,000 stores in 70 countries, that served as a global beacon for the manner in which a business can make extraordinary contributions to society—from empowering relationships with supplier-partners to major contributions to communities which are home to its shops. From her lips . . .

" The business of business should not be just about money. It should be about responsibility. It should be about public good, not private greed.

"Values carry the message of shared purpose, standards, and conceptions of what is worth living for and what is worth striving for. ▶

"My passionate belief is that business can be fun; it can be conducted with love and a powerful force for good.

"Get informed, get outraged, get inspired, get active.

"I want to work for a company that contributes to and is part of the community. I want something not just to invest in; I want something to believe in.

"Being good is good business.

"When you take the moral high ground it is difficult for anyone to object without sounding like a complete fool.

"Look at the Quakers. They were excellent business people who never lied, never stole; they cared for their employees and the community which gave them their wealth. They never took more money out than they put back in. ▶

"Running a company on market research is like driving while looking in the rearview mirror.

"Consumers have not been told effectively enough that they have huge power, and that purchasing and shopping involve a moral choice.

"All through history there have always been moments where business was not just about the accumulation of proceeds, but also for the public good. If I can't do something for the public good, what the hell am I doing?

"I believe in businesses where you engage in creative thinking and where you form some of your deepest relationships. If it isn't about the production of the human spirit, we are in big trouble. 🙶

Dame Anita Roddick, throughout her career

Enough.

The Vanguard Funds founder, the late Jack Bogle, father of no-load/no-fee index funds and arguably America's most successful investor for decades, wrote a brilliant book titled *Enough: True Measures of Money, Business, and Life*. It begins with this vignette from a party given by a billionaire on Shelter Island: "Kurt Vonnegut informs his pal Joseph Heller that their host, a hedge fund manager, had made more money in a single day than Heller had earned from his wildly popular novel *Catch-22* over its whole history. Heller responds, 'Yes, but I have something he will never have. . . enough.'" The heart of Bogle's book is captured by the chapter titles.

"Too Much Cost, Not Enough Value"

"Too Much Speculation, Not Enough Investment"

"Too Much Complexity, Not Enough Simplicity"

"Too Much Counting, Not Enough Trust"

"Too Much Business Conduct, Not Enough Professional Conduct" ▶

"Too Much Salesmanship, Not Enough Stewardship"

"Too Much Management, Not Enough Leadership"

"Too Much Focus on Things, Not Enough Focus on Commitment"

"Too Many Twenty-First Century Values, Not Enough Eighteenth-Century Values"

"Too Much 'Success,' Not Enough Character"

Long-Term Investors Prosper

4

Maximizing shareholder value 1970–?: The morally bankrupt, incomparably destructive economic idea that decapitated modern business and societal equity

Immediate personal gain > investment in the future

September 13, 1970:
Milton Friedman launches the "maximize shareholder value" movement in a business world where:

50% of corporate earnings goes to dividends/stock buybacks

50% goes to workers/R&D/capital investments

2012 (42 years later):
91% of corporate earnings goes to dividends/stock buybacks
(i.e.: the rich get even richer)

9% goes to workers/R&D/capital investments*

50%–50% to 91%–9% (!!!)

> " The very people we rely on to make investments in the productive capabilities that will increase our shared prosperity are instead devoting most of their companies' profits to uses that will increase their own prosperity. "

William Lazonick, "Profits Without Prosperity," *Harvard Business Review**

---

*Data here and in the introduction courtesy of William Lazonick.

2001–2015:

Of 615 companies representing 65% of market capitalization, 167 "had a long-term orientation."

" Long-term-focused companies surpassed their short-term-focused peers . . .

Average Company Revenue: +47%

Average Company Earnings: +36%

Average Company Economic Profit: +81%

Average Market Capitalization: +58%

Average Job Creation: +132% "

Dominic Barton, James Manyika, and Sarah Keohane
Williamson, "The Data: Where Long-Termism Pays Off,"
Harvard Business Review

5

People *Really* First

> " Business has to give people enriching, rewarding lives, or it's simply not worth doing. "

Richard Branson, *Business Stripped Bare: Adventures of a Global Entrepreneur**

---

*This quote is on Slide #1 of my 27-chapter, 4,096-slide presentation titled "The Works," available at excellencenow. com and tompeters.com. And this is also the data-proven best way to maximize mid- to long-term growth and profitability.

" The role of the director is to create a space where actors and actresses can become more than they have ever been before, more than they have ever dreamed of being. "

Robert Altman, Oscar-winning director

Leading:
The Pinnacle
of Human
Achievement

"Leading at any level: The greatest life opportunity one can have (literally); mid- to long-term success is no more and no less than a function of one's abiding attention to and effectiveness at helping team members grow and flourish as individuals and as contributing members of an energetic, self-renewing organization dedicated to the relentless pursuit of Excellence."

Tom Peters

" No matter what the situation, [every great manager's] first response is always to think about the individual concerned and how things can be arranged to help that individual experience success. "

Marcus Buckingham, *The One Thing You Need to Know . . . About Great Managing, Great Leading, and Sustained Individual Success*

**People.
Service.
Period.**

" An organization is:

People
(Leaders)

Serving People
(Frontline Team)

Serving People
(Customers/Communities) "

Tom Peters

> **If you want the staff to give great service to customers, the leaders have to give great service to the staff.**

Ari Weinzweig, cofounder of Zingerman's, *A Lapsed Anarchist's Approach to Building a Great Business*

" What employees experience,
Customers will. . . . Your
Customers will never be any
happier than your employees. "

John DiJulius, the DiJulius Group

" Nobody comes home after a surgery saying, 'Man, that was the best suturing I've ever seen!' or 'Sweet, they took out the correct kidney!'

Instead, we talk about the people who took care of us, the ones who coordinated the whole procedure—everyone from the receptionist to the nurses to the surgeon. And we don't just tell stories around the dinner table. We share our experiences through conversations with friends and colleagues and via social media sites like Facebook and Twitter. 〞

Paul Spiegelman and Britt Berrett, from the chapter "What Does Come First?" in *Patients Come Second: Leading Change by Changing the Way You Lead*

Hiring = #1

> " In short, hiring is the most important aspect of business and yet remains woefully misunderstood. "

Philip Delves Broughton, "The Hard Work of Getting Ahead," *Wall Street Journal*

**Empathy/
Emotional
Intelligence
100% (!!!) of Jobs**

> " The ultimate filter we use [in the hiring process] is that we only hire nice people. . . .
>
> I believe in culture so strongly and that one bad apple can spoil the bunch. "

Peter Miller in Adam Bryant's "Peter Miller of Optinose: To Work Here, Win the 'Nice' Vote," *New York Times* (Candidates for even the most technical jobs in this biotech company must interview with people of all ranks and disciplines to test the "nice" fit. All interviewers have veto power.)

Hire more liberal arts grads.

Regardless of industry.
Now.

Underpins "people focus."
Underpins (and "overpins") design-mindedness,
the #1 enterprise differentiator.
In general adds humanity in businesses which feature
MBAs and engineers.
Best defense against the AI tsunami.

" At graduation, business and professional degree holders in general (MBAs, engineers, lawyers, and so on) have higher interview and hire rates, and higher starting salaries, than new liberal arts grads.

By year 20, liberal arts grads have risen farther than their biz-professional degree holder peers. ▶

At one giant tech firm,
43 percent of liberal arts grads
had made it to upper-middle
management compared to
32 percent of engineering grads.

At one giant financial services
firm, 60 percent of the worst
managers, according to company
evaluations, had MBAs, while
60 percent of the best had
only BAs. **"**

Henry Mintzberg, from research cited in *Managers Not MBAs: A Hard Look at the Soft Practice of Managing and Management Development*

Read ...

The Fuzzy and the Techie: Why the Liberal Arts Will Rule the Digital World, by Scott Hartley

You Can Do Anything: The Surprising Power of a "Useless" Liberal Arts Education, by George Anders

Sensemaking: The Power of the Humanities in the Age of the Algorithm, by Christian Madsbjerg

Range: Why Generalists Triumph in a Specialized World, by David Epstein

" When we talk about the qualities we want in people, empathy is a big one. If you can empathize with people, then you can do a good job. If you have no ability to empathize, . . . then it's difficult to help people improve. "

Stewart Butterfield in Adam Bryant's "Stewart Butterfield of Slack: Is Empathy on Your Résumé?," *New York Times*

" We look for people that are warm and caring and actually altruistic. We look for people who have a fun-loving attitude. "

Colleen Barrett, president emeritus, Southwest Airlines

Hire the Quiet Ones

Frequently (and stupidly) neglected . . . "Quiet power."

Hire quiet.

Promote quiet.

Noisy people are not the most creative people.

Noisy people are not the best salespeople.

Noisy people are not the best leaders.

" The Extrovert Ideal has been documented in many studies. . . . Talkative people, for example, are rated as smarter, better-looking, more interesting, and more desirable as friends.

Velocity of speech counts as well as volume: we rank fast talkers as more competent and likable than slow ones. . . . But we make a grave mistake to embrace the Extrovert Ideal so unthinkingly. "

▶

Limits to Assertiveness

" Also remember the dangers of the New Groupthink.

If it's creativity you're after, ask your employees to solve problems alone before sharing their ideas. . . . Don't mistake assertiveness or eloquence for good ideas. "

> The next time you see a person with a composed face and a soft voice, remember that inside her mind she might be solving an equation, composing a sonnet, designing a hat. She might, that is, be deploying the powers of quiet. **"**

Susan Cain, *Quiet: The Power of Introverts in a World That Can't Stop Talking*

(FYI: *Quiet* is my pick as best business book of the century to date. For heaven's sake, we are talking about no less than our implicit bias against almost half of the population. And the fact that the underattended half, once given the chance, more often than not outperform their noisy peers! Susan Cain made me feel like an idiot for never having paid attention to this!)

Promotion Decisions:
Life and Death

[Promotions] are life-and-death decisions.

Peter F. Drucker, *The Practice of Management*

Training =
Corporate
Investment #1

> " training, TRAINING
> and M-O-R-E
> T-R-A-I-N-I-N-G* "

Admiral Chester Nimitz, commander in chief, Pacific Ocean Area, in *Neptune's Inferno: The U.S. Navy at Guadalcanal* by James D. Hornfischer (Capitalization and punctuation are Nimitz's.)

---

*The U.S. Navy was woefully underprepared at the time of Pearl Harbor. Fix? First and foremost: T-R-A-I-N-I-N-G. *Training was more important than hardware/more ships*, per Nimitz.

Training Is a Capital Investment . . .

NOT an "Expense"!

> "If you don't think training is of paramount importance (Capital Investment #1), ask a Navy admiral, an Army or Air Force or USMC general, a football coach, an archery coach, a fire chief, a police chief, a theater director, a symphony conductor, a pilot, the boss of an ER or ICU, the operations chief of a nuclear power plant, a great restaurateur, a public speaker (me) . . ."

Tom Peters

"Give me six hours to chop down a tree, and I will spend the first four sharpening the axe."

Abraham Lincoln

Frontline Leaders = Corporate Asset #1

" In great armies, the job of generals is to back up their sergeants. "

Colonel Thomas Wilhelm, in Robert D. Kaplan's "The Man Who Would Be Khan," *Atlantic*

Frontline Leaders Are . . .

1. Do you absolutely understand and act upon the fact that the frontline leader is the key leadership role in the organization?

2. Do the people professionals (and top management in general) single out frontline bosses individually and collectively for special developmental attention?

3. Do you spend gobs and gobs (and gobs) of time selecting frontline supervisors?

4. Are you willing, pain notwithstanding, to leave a frontline supervisor slot open until you can fill it with somebody spectacular?

5. Do you have the absolute best training and continuing development programs in the industry for frontline supervisors?

6. Do you formally and rigorously and continuously mentor frontline supervisors?

7. Are your frontline supervisors accorded the attention and acknowledgment and respect that their position merits?

6

**People *Really* First:
Radical Inclusion**

Enterprise Success = More Women in Charge

> " If you educate a man, you simply educate an individual, but if you educate a woman, you educate a nation. "

James Emman Kwegyir Aggrey

" **If you want something said, ask a man; if you want something done, ask a woman.** "

Margaret Thatcher, former prime minister, UK

" Research [by McKinsey & Co.] suggests that, in order to succeed, companies should start by promoting more women. "

Nicholas Kristof, "Twitter, Women, and Power," *New York Times*

> "As Leaders, Women Rule: New studies find that female managers outshine their male counterparts on almost every measure."

Rochelle Sharpe, *Bloomberg Businessweek*

> "Women are rated higher in fully 12 of 16 competencies that go into outstanding leadership.
>
> And two of the traits where women outscored men to the highest degree—taking initiative and driving for results—have long been thought of as particularly male strengths."

Jack Zenger and Joseph Folkman, "Are Women Better Leaders Than Men?," *Harvard Business Review*

" The five-year study [of 2,482 managers from 459 organizations] . . . shows significant differences in the leadership skill levels practiced by male and female managers.

Employees rated female managers higher than male managers in seventeen of the twenty skill areas assessed, fifteen at a statistically significant level. Bosses rated female managers higher than male managers in sixteen of the twenty skill areas, all sixteen at a statistically significant level. **"**

Lawrence A. Pfaff & Associates study, "A Women's Place? In Charge," *Businessweek*

Women's Blue-Ribbon Skills at Investment

Warren Buffett Invests Like a Girl: And Why You Should, Too

by LouAnn Lofton

Women . . .

- Trade less than men do
- Exhibit less overconfidence—more likely to know what they don't know
- Shun risk more than male investors do
- Are less optimistic, more realistic than their male counterparts
- Put in more time and effort researching possible investments—consider details and alternate points of view
- Are more immune to peer pressure—tend to make decisions the same way regardless of who's watching
- Learn from their mistakes

" When women get involved in finances, they do better than men, because men focus on a shorter-term performance, while women take a longer view. "

Kathy Murphy, president, Fidelity Investments, manager of $1.7 trillion in assets, in *TheStreet*

Women "link rather than rank [workers]; favour interactive-collaborative leadership styles [empowerment beats top-down decision making]; are comfortable sharing information; see redistribution of power as victory, not surrender; readily accept ambiguity; honour intuition as well as rationality; are inherently flexible; appreciate cultural diversity. "

Judy B. Rosener, summarized by Hilarie Owen, *Creating Leaders in the Classroom*

Boards: 50% women within 36 months.

Executive teams: 50% women within 36 months.

Quit screwing around.

Universal Inclusivity:
Every Action, Every Decision

" I appreciate your Black Lives Matter post.

Now follow that up with a picture of your senior management team and your board. "

Brickson Diamond, CEO, diversity consulting firm Big Answers

" Dear white corporate America,

I get it. I know you have the best intentions. . . . You want to do the right thing. But you just don't know how. . . . The fact that you're only asking now is part of the problem. . . .

Listen to your Black employees. They've been sounding the alarm for years. But don't stop there. Dig into the cold, hard Black data. Learn where Black people exist in your company—and more importantly, where they don't. Count the too-few Black faces in meetings. Notice the muted Black voices in conversations where decisions get made. If you do that, you'll see the problem clear as day. . . .

You can fix this. . . . ▶

Inside your company walls, you need to hire more Black people. Period.

On one side of the equation, that means fixing the 'pipeline' challenge, once and for all. So, redouble your efforts to recruit, attract, develop, and elevate Black talent. Fund educational institutions that champion Black kids and their futures.

On the other side of the equation, that means helping Black talent climb the ladder, and turning over power and authority to rising Black leaders. Retention and promotion is just as urgent as recruiting and hiring. . . .

Analyze where you are as an organization. Set goals for where you want to be. Put in place incentives to achieve those goals. Measure against them ruthlessly and relentlessly. **"**

From a full-page *New York Times* statement by Omar Johnson, founder, ØPUS United and former Marketing VP at Apple

Extreme Humanism: Design That Makes the World a Better Place

Extreme Humanism:

World-Enhancing Design/Products and Services That Brighten Our Lives* **

Value-Added Differentiator #1***

> **"** Expose yourself to the best things that humans have done. And then try to bring those things into what you are doing. **"**

Steve Jobs in Steve Denning's "The Lost Interview: Steve Jobs Tells Us What Really Matters," *Forbes*

---

*You say, "'World-enhancing' is a tall order."
I say, "Yup. Why else bother?"
**Applies as much to a new training course as to a new customer offering.
***10× more important as AI engulfs us.

"The peculiar grace of a Shaker chair is due to the fact that it was made by someone capable of believing that an angel might come and sit on it. "

Thomas Merton in *Religion in Wood: A Book of Shaker Furniture* by Edward Deming Andrews and Faith Andrews

> " He said for him the craft of building a boat was like a religion. You had to give yourself up to it spiritually; you had to surrender yourself absolutely to it. When you were done and walked away, you had to feel that you had left a piece of yourself behind in it forever, a bit of your heart. "

Daniel James Brown, on George Yeoman Pocock, premier racing shell designer-builder, *The Boys in the Boat: Nine Americans and Their Epic Quest for Gold at the 1936 Berlin Olympics*

" In some way, by caring, we are actually serving humanity. . . .

People might think it's a stupid belief, but it's a goal—it's a contribution that we hope we can make, in some small way, to culture. 99

Jony Ive, former Apple design chief, in Ian Parker's "The Shape of Things to Come," *New Yorker*

"Every business school in the world would flunk you if you came out with a business plan that said, 'Oh, by the way, we're going to design and fabricate our own screws at an exponentially higher cost than it would cost to buy them.'

But these aren't just screws. Like the [Nest] thermometer itself, they're better screws, epic screws, screws with, dare I say it, deeper meaning. Functionally, they utilize a specific thread pattern that allows them to go into nearly any surface, from wood to plaster to thin sheet metal. And the [custom] screwdriver feels balanced to the hand. It has the Nest logo on it and looks 'Nest-y,' just like everything from Apple looks 'Apple-y.' **99**

Tony Fadell, Nest founder, in Rich Karlgaard's *The Soft Edge: Where Great Companies Find Lasting Success*

Touch-Taste-Smell-Smile

" Leave a bit of your heart behind"

"Epic screws, screws with deeper meaning"

"Believe that an angel might come and sit on it"

"Jony [Ive] and Steve [Jobs] would discuss corners for hours upon hours"

"Serve humanity by caring"

"Bring the best things humans have done into what you are doing"

"No new vehicle (MINI Cooper S)
  has provoked more smiles"

"Religion"

"Romance"

"Fundamental soul"

"Emotion eats reason for breakfast"

"Seeking a Business Romantic"

"Create something greater than yourself"

"Express our gratitude and our love for humanity 99

Thoughts on design, sources various

Tim Leberecht authored the insightful book *The Business Romantic: Give Everything, Quantify Nothing, and Create Something Greater Than Yourself.*

At one point, Leberecht suggests that an enterprise needs a formally designated "Business Romantic." To add life to the idea, he placed the following ad on Craigslist:

Seeking Business Romantic to Join Our Team

Reporting to the CEO, the Business Romantic will help colleagues, customers, partners, and society at large see the beauty of the business world with fresh eyes. Embracing hope as a strategy, the Business Romantic presents cohesive narratives that make sense of ever more complex and fragmented workplace and market conversations. Instead of focusing on assets and return-on-investment, the Business Romantic exposes the hidden treasures of business and delivers return-on-community. The Business Romantic develops, designs, and implements "acts of significance" that restore nostalgic trust in business as the most impactful human enterprise and provide internal and external audiences with brand and workplace experiences rich with meaning, delight, and fun. We're looking for a self-starter with strong entrepreneurial drive, exquisite taste, and a proven track record of managing the immeasurable. Specific responsibilities will include but are not limited to:

▶

- Carving out spaces for the artful and playful at work
- Elevating day-to-day interactions and transactions to experiences "greater than ourselves"
- Finding meaning in the seemingly mundane
- Shifting organizational and brand cultures from utilitarian/transactional to generous/transcendent
- Creating zones of discomfort and "critical events" that replace convenience with friction
- Doing things for no reason and taking part in joyous, aimless activities such as mystery meetings or result-free conversations
- Conceiving of and implementing passion projects
- Going on regular hikes with the CFO
- Providing leadership to other romantics at the workplace 99

Leberecht reports that there were hundreds of fascinating responses.

Extreme Humanism:

Small > Big*

> " Courtesies of a small and trivial character are the ones which strike deepest to the grateful and appreciating heart. "

Henry Clay

---

*Replace your "big-or-bust" fixation with an all-hands, warp-speed "small"-fixation culture; I call it a "TGR-ing culture," where one and all focus on continuously adding TGRs (Things Gone Right).

" Let's not forget that small emotions are the great captains of our lives. "

Vincent van Gogh

> " We don't remember the days,
> we remember the moments. "

Cesare Pavese

Small > Big:

A (Tiny) Patient Photo, an 80% More Accurate Evaluation

A Mirror as Big as a Band-Aid

" For the study [presented to the Radiological Society of North America], 318 patients referred for CT agreed to be photographed prior to the exam. . . . The photograph appeared automatically when a patient's file was opened.

After interpreting the results of the exams, 15 radiologists were given questionnaires. . . . All 15 radiologists admitted feeling more empathy towards the patients after viewing their photos. . . . More importantly, the results showed that radiologists provided a more meticulous reading of medical image results when a photo of the patient accompanied the file. ▶

Incidental findings are unexpected abnormalities found on an image that may have health implications beyond the scope of the original exam. In order to assess the effect of the photographs on interpretation, 81 examinations with incidental findings were shown in a blinded fashion to the same radiologists three months later but without the photos. Approximately 80 percent of the radiologic incidental findings reported originally were not reported when the photograph was omitted from the file. 99

Radiological Society of North America, "Patient Photos Spur Radiologist Empathy and Eye for Detail," *ScienceDaily*
(Note: Typically, radiologists interpreting results have no direct patient contact—often, they are a continent or so away.)

" Janet Dugan, a healthcare architect, took inspiration from her recent experience having an MRI (Magnetic Resonance Image) scan. While she was lying still and waiting, she noticed a small mirror that had been placed below the head support piece. It was angled so that she could see through the barrel to the radiology technician and make eye contact with him. 'What a small thing,' she told me. 'And yet what a difference it made. I felt less alone. I was connected to another person at the very moment I needed support.

And even though I'm not claustrophobic, it calmed me some to be able to see out of the barrel. . . . I [saw] that the technician was friendly and that the nurse went out of her way to make me laugh. . . . I firmly believe in the power of design to contribute to the healing process—that architecture can shape events and transform lives. But that day, in that experience, the thing that really gave me comfort was a tiny mirror about as big as a Band-Aid.' 🙸

Tim Leberecht, *The Business Romantic: Give Everything, Quantify Nothing, and Create Something Greater Than Yourself*

Design Is
Everything.

> " Design is everything.
> Everything is design.
> We are all designers. "

Richard Farson, *The Power of Design: A Force for Transforming Everything*

> " Only one company can be the cheapest. All others must use design. "

Rodney Fitch, Fitch+Co., *Retail Design*

Compete with the immortals! "

David Ogilvy, *Ogilvy on Advertising*

Deloitte Research Discovers Just Three Rules for Success

Deloitte researches "Excellence"

25,000 companies assessed
45 years of data
344 exceptional performers
27 superstar "best of the best"

Attributes of the "best of the best"

Better before cheaper.

Revenue before cost.

There are no other rules.

Michael E. Raynor and Mumtaz Ahmed, *The Three Rules: How Exceptional Companies Think* (This is research of the most profound sort.)

We are defined by design.

Design is spirit.

Design is soul.

Design is heart.

Sustainability:
The Right Thing to Do.
The Profitable Thing to Do.

Sustainability:

" It's the right thing to do, it's the smart thing to do, it's the profitable thing to do. "

L. Hunter Lovins, Rocky Mountain Institute and Natural Capitalism Solutions

"Buy less, choose well, make it last. Quality rather than quantity: That is true sustainability. If people only bought beautiful things rather than rubbish, we wouldn't have climate change! "

Vivienne Westwood, fashion designer

" What is clear is that many of our conventions and practices are no longer valid for the context in which we now find ourselves. . . .

A multitude of social and environmental indicators make it only too apparent that contemporary production systems and consumption patterns are physically, ethically, and spiritually untenable. And so we must move forward into unknown territory and explore new approaches that are more environmentally benign and personally and socially enriching. 99

Stuart Walker, *Sustainable by Design: Explorations in Theory and Practice*

The World's Top Two (Underserved) Markets:

Women Buy (Almost) Everything.

"Oldies" Have (Almost) All the Money.

Women Buy (Almost) Everything.

Women are the majority market."

Fara Warner, *The Power of the Purse: How Smart Businesses Are Adapting to the World's Most Important Consumers—Women*

> "Forget China, India, and the internet: economic growth is driven by women. "

"The Importance of Sex," *The Economist*

"Women now drive the global economy.

They control $20 trillion in consumer spending, and that figure could climb to $28 trillion [within five years]. . . . In aggregate, women represent a growth market bigger than China and India combined—more in fact than twice as big as China and India combined. . . . "

Michael J. Silverstein and Kate Sayre, "The Female Economy," *Harvard Business Review*

" One thing is certain: Women's rise to power, which is linked to the increase in wealth per capita, is happening in all domains and at all levels of society. . . .

This is just the beginning. The phenomenon will only grow as girls prove to be more successful than boys in the school system.

For a number of observers, we have already entered the age of 'womenomics,' the economy as thought out and practiced by a woman. 🙶

Aude Zieseniss de Thuin, "Women Are Drivers of Global Growth," *Financial Times*

Women are drivers of global growth 99

Aude Zieseniss de Thuin, "Women Are Drivers of Global Growth," *Financial Times*

"Oldies" Have (Almost) All the Money.

> "'Age Power' will rule the 21st century, and we are woefully unprepared."

Ken Dychtwald, *Age Power: How the 21st Century Will Be Ruled by the New Old*

> "The New Customer Majority [age 44–65] is the only adult market with realistic prospects for significant sales growth in dozens of product lines for thousands of companies."

David B. Wolfe and Robert E. Snyder, *Ageless Marketing: Strategies for Reaching the Hearts and Minds of the New Customer Majority*

"Households headed by someone 40 or older enjoy 91% of our population's net worth. . . . The mature market is the dominant market in the U.S. economy, making the majority of expenditures in virtually every category."

Carol M. Morgan and Doran J. Levy, *Marketing to the Mindset of Boomers and Their Elders: Using Psychographics and More to Identify and Reach Your Best Targets*

People turning 50 today have half their adult lives ahead of them. ""

Bill Novelli, former CEO of AARP, *50+: Igniting a Revolution to Reinvent America*

"Older people have an image problem. As a culture, we're conditioned toward youth. . . . When we think of youth . . . we think 'energetic and colorful;' when we think of middle age or 'mature,' we think 'tired and washed out.' And when we think of 'old' or 'senior,' we think either 'exhausted and gray' or, more likely, we just don't think.

The financial numbers are absolutely inarguable—the Mature Market has the money. Yet advertisers remain astonishingly indifferent to them. "

Martha Barletta, *PrimeTime Women: How to Win the Hearts, Minds, and Business of Boomer Big Spenders*

> " Oldies don't 'have the money.'
> They (we!) have ALL the money. "

Tom Peters

B+W =
APP+LTL

Boomers + Women =
All the Purchasing Power + Lotsa Time Left

Big
Stinks/
SMEs Rule

" I am often asked by would-be entrepreneurs seeking escape from life within huge corporate structures,

'How do I build a small firm for myself?' The answer seems obvious: buy a very large one and just wait. "

Paul Ormerod, *Why Most Things Fail: Evolution, Extinction and Economics*

> " Research shows that new, small companies create almost all the new private sector jobs—and are disproportionately innovative. "

Gervais Williams, "If Small is the Future then We Will All be Big Winners" *Financial Times*

> " 64% GDP.
> 62% total employment.
> 78% new job creation. "

Joseph H. Astrachan and Melissa Carey Shanker, *"Family Businesses' Contribution to the U.S. Economy: A Closer Look"* (Kennesaw State University)

Big, Uh, Stinks

> " I don't believe in economies of scale. You don't get better by being bigger.
>
> You get worse. "

Dick Kovacevich, retired CEO, Wells Fargo

" Mr. Foster and his McKinsey colleagues collected detailed performance data stretching back 40 years for 1,000 [large/public] U.S. companies.

They found that NONE of the long-term survivors managed to outperform the market.

Worse, the longer companies had been in the database, the worse they did. **"**

Simon London, "Long-term survival of the not so fit," *Financial Times*

" Multinational companies, the agents behind global integration, were already in retreat well before the populist revolts of 2016. Their financial performance has slipped so that they are no longer outstripping local firms.

Many seem to have exhausted their ability to cut costs and taxes and to out-think their local competitors . . . . Central to the rise of the global firm was its claim to be a superior moneymaking machine.

That claim lies in tatters. 99

"The Multinational Company Is in Trouble," *The Economist*

"Almost every personal friend I have in the world works on Wall Street.

You can buy and sell the same company six times and everybody makes money, but I'm not sure we're actually innovating. . . . "

Jeff Immelt, former CEO, GE

"When asked recently to name just one big merger that has lived up to expectations, Leon Cooperman, the former cochairman of Goldman Sachs's investment policy committee, answered:

'I'm sure that there are success stories out there, but at this moment I draw a blank.'"

Mark L. Sirower, *The Synergy Trap*

" Not a single company that qualified as having made a sustained transformation ignited its leap with a big acquisition or merger. Moreover, comparison companies—those that failed to make a leap or, if they did, failed to sustain it—often tried to make themselves great with a big . . . acquisition or merger.

They failed to grasp the simple truth that while you can buy your way to growth, you cannot buy your way to greatness. 99

Jim Collins, "The Merger Mystery," *Time*

SME Superstars

The Basement Mold Removal Champs

Excellence Anywhere and Everywhere

" Basement Systems Inc. of Seymour, Conn., is primarily in the business of getting mold and dampness out of basements. Your home's once foul and perhaps poisonous but now rejuvenated lower reaches become fit for storage or use as a family room or extra bedroom; that is, effectively adding a room to your house. (No small thing, eh?) ▶

"'Basement improvement.'
What a 'dreary business'?
Not to Larry Janesky!
For Larry J. and his spirited crew:
Basements rock!

"Among many other things, Janesky codified his activities and the value thereof in his book *Dry Basement Science*—which sold over 100,000 copies. He also holds 27 patents. Started in 1986, the fast-growing company has at last look 400 dealers in six countries and revenue exceeds $100 million.

"Basement Systems is also a consistent prize winner (local, state, national) in categories such as 'Best Places to Work,' 'Best Small Business,' and 'Entrepreneur of the Year.' The company is a paragon on just about any dimension you can name. 99

From *The Excellence Dividend* and *Excellence Now: Extreme Humanism;* and *Dry Basement Science* by Larry Janesky

It Ain't Just Another Garage

"Carchitecture" at 1111 Lincoln Road

That address has become a Miami Beach landmark. For example, LeBron James, then with the Miami Heat and the world's best basketball player, introduced his 11th Nike shoe, celebrated with hoopla of the first order, at . . . 1111 Lincoln Road. ▶

Just what is this address?
A 300-car parking garage!

Developer Robert Wennett wanted
to reintroduce the original vision
of Lincoln Road, set back in 1910.
Among many other things, that
meant having a makeover designed
by the world-renowned Swiss
architects Herzog & de Meuron.
The "product" amounted to, per one
member of the press, "carchitecture,"
an "unimaginable marriage of high-
end architecture and car storage."

1111 Lincoln features, among many other things, public art and a grand staircase (joggers by the score work out there every morning—many then move on to in-garage yoga classes). Wennett calls it a curated space that provides an experience, telling a story.

Is this "over the top"? Of course. But it is also a very profitable venture, a community-changer, and a peerless demonstration of SME excellence.

Derived from (*Fast Company* cofounder) William C. Taylor's book *Simply Brilliant: How Great Organizations Do Ordinary Things in Extraordinary Ways*

The Shape and Contributions of the Winning SMEs

Inc. magazine cofounder Bo Burlingham wrote a remarkable book titled *Small Giants: Companies That Chose to Be Great Instead of Big*

The 14 featured top performers shared four traits: ▶

1. "They cultivated exceptionally intimate relationships with customers and suppliers, based on personal contact, one-on-one interaction, and mutual commitment to delivering on promises."

2. "Each company had an extraordinarily intimate relationship with the local city, town, or county in which it did business—a relationship that went well beyond the usual concept of 'giving back.'"

3. "The companies also had what struck me as unusually intimate workplaces."

4. "I noticed the passion that the leaders brought to what the company did. They loved the subject matter, whether it be music, safety lighting, food, special effects, engineering, beer, records storage, construction, dining, or fashion."

Innovation:
Most Tries
Wins

Innovation Bedrock #1:

Try the Most Stuff

> " We have a strategic plan—it's called doing things. "
>
> Herb Kelleher, Southwest Airlines founder

" We made mistakes, of course. Most of them were omissions we didn't think of when we initially wrote the software. We fixed them by doing it over and over, again and again.

We do the same today. While our competitors are still sucking their thumbs trying to make the design perfect, we've already gone through five rounds of testing. By the time our rivals are ready to begin development, we are on version No. 10. It gets back to planning versus acting: We act from day one; others plan how to plan—for months. 🙶

Michael R. Bloomberg, *Bloomberg by Bloomberg*

" WTTMSW: Whoever Tries The Most Stuff Wins. "

Tom Peters

" WTTMS(ASTMSUTF)W: Whoever Tries The Most Stuff (And Screws The Most Stuff Up The Fastest) Wins. "

Tom Peters

Innovation
Bedrock #2:
Serious Play

> **"** Serious play is not an oxymoron; it is the essence of innovation. . . . You can't be a serious innovator unless you are willing and able to play. **"**

Michael Schrage, *Serious Play: How the World's Best Companies Simulate to Innovate*

> **"** I want a 'sandbox partner.' **"**

Elliott Masie, e-learning pioneer

Innovation Bedrock #3:
"Fail. Forward. Fast."

"Fail faster. Succeed sooner. "

David Kelley, IDEO founder

"Fail. Forward. Fast. "

High-tech executive, Philadelphia, at one of
Tom's speeches

Try again. Fail again. Fail better. 🙼

Samuel Beckett, *Worstward Ho*

Reward excellent failures.
Punish mediocre successes. "

Phil Daniels, Australian executive who attended one of Tom's seminars, regarding "the six words that underpin my company's success"

" We normally shoot a few takes, even if the first one was terrific, because what I'm really hoping for is a 'mistake.' I think that most of the really great moments in my films were not planned. They were things that occurred and we thought, 'Wow, look at that—that's something we want to keep!' That's where you hit the truth button with the audience. "

Robert Altman when asked how, when filming, he knew when enough was enough

Innovation Bedrock #4: Variety Is the Spice of Success

Diversity Trumps Ability

" It is hardly possible to overrate the value . . . of placing human beings in contact with persons dissimilar to themselves, and with modes of thought and action unlike those with which they are familiar. . . . Such communication has always been, and is peculiarly in the present age, one of the primary sources of progress. "

John Stuart Mill, *Principles of Political Economy*

> "Diverse groups of problem solvers—groups of people with diverse tools—consistently outperformed groups of the best and the brightest. If I formed two groups, one random (and therefore diverse) and one consisting of the best individual performers, the first group almost always did better. . . . Diversity trumped ability."

Scott E. Page, *The Difference: How the Power of Diversity Creates Better Groups, Firms, Schools, and Societies*

" Recently a young mother asked for advice. What, she wanted to know, was she to do with a 7-year-old who was obstreperous, outspoken and inconveniently willful? 'Keep her,' I replied. . . . [The] suffragists refused to be polite in demanding what they wanted or grateful for getting what they deserved. Works for me. "

Anna Quindlen, "To Hell with Well Behaved," *Newsweek*

Innovation Bedrock #5: "Learn Not to Be Careful"

I'm uncomfortable when
I'm comfortable. 99

Jay Chiat, "Jay's Way," *Communication Arts*

Learn not to be careful.

Photographer Diane Arbus to her students

> Alice laughed. 'There's no use trying,' she said: 'one *can't* believe impossible things.' 'I daresay you haven't had much practice,' said the Queen. 'When I was your age, I always did it for half an hour a day. Why, sometimes I've believed as many as six impossible things before breakfast.'

Lewis Carroll, *Through the Looking-Glass: And What Alice Found There*

Leadership:
You Must
Care

Culture *Is* the Game

"If I could have chosen not to tackle the IBM culture head-on, I probably wouldn't have. . . . My bias coming in was toward strategy, analysis, and measurement. . . . In comparison, changing the attitude and behavior of hundreds of thousands of people is very, very hard."

"I came to see, in my time at IBM, that culture isn't just one aspect of the game—it *is* the game."

Louis V. Gerstner, Jr., *Who Says Elephants Can't Dance? Inside IBM's Historic Turnaround* (Gerstner, in his McKinsey days, was wholly dismissive of my focus on "the soft stuff.")

" **Culture eats strategy for breakfast.** "

Edgar H. Schein, MIT professor

Q:

"What matters most to a company over time? Strategy or culture?"

A:

"Culture."

Dominic Barton, managing director, McKinsey & Co., responding to reporter Dennis K. Berman in "Managing McKinsey Through Scandal," *Wall Street Journal*

" CEO's First Commandment: CEO Job #1 is setting—and micro-nourishing, one day, one hour, one minute at a time— an effective people-truly-first, innovate-or-die, excellence-or-bust corporate culture. "

Tom Peters

" MBWA: Managing By Wandering Around "

Courtesy Hewlett-Packard

MBWA was the animating force for *In Search of Excellence*; that is, business leaders not absorbed by abstractions represented in a strategic plan or voluminous financials, but business leaders, instead, as real people, in the field, in intimate touch with the real work and those who perform that real work.

It was 1979. The research for what became *In Search of Excellence* was in its infancy. On the list of potential featured companies was the relatively youthful, innovative firm called Hewlett-Packard. An interview was subsequently arranged with HP president John Young in his Palo Alto "office"—a small cubicle. (Hmmmmm. Not the presidential norm.) At some point in the exchange, the term "MBWA" spilled out of his mouth. I didn't know it then, but, no joke, as of that utterance, everything changed in my professional life. Mr. Young's MBWA meant and means . . . Managing By Wandering Around. Literally. You can't lead from your office/cubicle or via messaging or emailing or PowerPointing or spreadsheeting. You lead, if you are serious about creating an energized human-humane organization, by routine, live interaction "at the coalface."

" MBWA: FUN . . . or you're in the wrong job. "

Tom Peters

To be sure, via MBWA you learn close-up what's really going on. But there's more, much more. It came like a flash during a beach walk in New Zealand, 35 years after *In Search of Excellence*: You do MBWA because it's, yes, *fun*. It's a delight, or should be, to be out in the work spaces with the folks who are on your team who wrestle with day-to-day problems. It's fun to exchange stories. You learn important "stuff," certainly. But that's just 5 percent of it. The rest is about camaraderie in a human organization/community. I'm tough-minded about this ultra-"soft" activity: If you *don't* deeply enjoy being around and intimately engaging with your folks; if you *don't* deeply enjoy chatting up the distribution team at 1:00 a.m., I sincerely suggest you find something else to do with your life. (Sorry.)

MBZA: Managing By Zooming Around

MBWA is shorthand for the effective leader's intimacy with the real work of the organization. During the pandemic, traditional MBWA went out the window. And the "new normal," pre- and post-pandemic, will be and is marked by a dramatic increase in remote work. Yet the MBWA concept is as important as ever. I call a significant share of leader connection amid the new normal MBZA, Managing By Zooming Around. There will of course be Zoom meetings. But beyond that, many leaders are engaging in a steady diet of one-on-one MBZA. For most, the awkwardness of the new routine quickly goes away. But the big point here is that the MBWA concept is more important than ever—and with remote work increasingly the norm, some new form(s) of up-close-and-personal interaction must become a centerpiece of your daily activities.

Listening Is . . .

> " The best way to persuade others is with your ears, by listening to them. "

Former U.S. Secretary of State Dean Rusk

> " Never miss a good chance to shut up. "

Will Rogers

" Listening is . . . the ultimate mark of *Respect*.

Listening is . . . the heart and soul of *Engagement*.

Listening is . . . the heart and soul of *Kindness*.

Listening is . . . the heart and soul of *Thoughtfulness*.

Listening is . . . the basis for true *Collaboration*.

Listening is . . . the basis for true *Partnership*.

Listening is . . . a *Developable Individual Skill*.

(Though women are far better at it than men.)

Listening is . . . the basis for *Community*.

Listening is . . . the bedrock of *Joint Ventures that work*.

Listening is . . . the bedrock of *Joint Ventures that last*.

Listening is . . . the core of *effective Cross-functional Communication*.

▶

Listening is . . . the engine of *superior EXECUTION*.

Listening is . . . the key to *making the Sale*.

Listening is . . . the key to *Keeping the Customer's Business*.

Listening is . . . the engine of *Network development*.

Listening is . . . *Learning*.

Listening is . . . the *sine qua non of Renewal*.

Listening is . . . the *sine qua non of Creativity*.

Listening is . . . the core of *taking Diverse opinions aboard.*

Listening is . . . *Strategy.*

Listening is . . . *Source #1 of "Value-added."*

Listening is . . . *the principal basis for extreme humanism.*

Listening is . . . *Profitable.*

Listening is . . . *the Commitment to EXCELLENCE.*

If you agree with the above, shouldn't listening be . . . *a Core Value*? **"**

Tom Peters

Aggressive
Listening

"My education in leadership really began when I was in Washington, watching [Defense Secretary] William Perry in action. He was universally loved and admired by heads of state . . . and by our own and our allies' troops. A lot of that was because of the way he listened. Each person who talked to him had his complete, undivided attention. Everyone blossomed in his presence, because he was so respectful, and I realized I wanted to affect people the same way. Perry became my role model, but that wasn't enough to change my leadership style. Something bigger had to happen, and it did. ▶

It was painful, but crucial for my realization, that listening doesn't always come naturally to me. . . . How many times, I asked myself, had I barely glanced up from my work when a subordinate came into my office? . . . I vowed to treat every encounter with every person on the ship [Abrashoff was captain of the *USS Benfold*] as the most important thing at that moment. . . . I decided that my job was to listen aggressively. **99**

Captain D. Michael Abrashoff, *It's Your Ship: Management Techniques from the Best Damn Ship in the Navy*

Fierce Listening

" It's amazing how this seemingly small thing—simply paying fierce attention to another, really asking, really listening, even during a brief conversation—can evoke such a wholehearted response. "

Susan Scott, *Fierce Conversations: Achieving Success at Work and in Life, One Conversation at a Time*

The Power of Perceived Self-Control

Adult subjects were given some complex puzzles to solve and a proofreading chore.

In the background was a loud, randomly occurring distracting noise; to be specific, it was a 'combination of two people speaking Spanish, one speaking Armenian, a mimeograph machine running, a desk calculator, and a typewriter, and street noise—producing a composite, nondistinguishable roar.' ▶

The subjects were split into two groups. Individuals in one set were just told to work at the task. Individuals in the other were provided with a button to push to turn off the noise, a 'modern analog of control—the off switch.'

The group with the off switch solved five times the number of puzzles as their cohorts and made but a tiny fraction of the number of proofreading errors.

Now for the kicker . . . none of the subjects in the off switch group ever used the switch. The mere knowledge that one can exert control made the difference. **"**

Herbert Lefcourt's experiment from *Locus of Control: Current Trends in Theory and Research*

There's
A-L-W-A-Y-S
Time for
Relationship
Building!!!

" Personal relationships are the fertile soil from which *all* advancement, *all* success, *all* achievement in real life grows. "

Ben Stein, investment guru

> " The capacity to develop close and enduring relationships is one mark of a leader. Unfortunately, many leaders of major companies believe their job is to create the strategy, organization structure, and organizational processes. Then they just delegate the work to be done, remaining aloof from the people doing the work. "

Bill George, *Authentic Leadership: Rediscovering the Secrets to Creating Lasting Value* (former CEO of Medtronic)

The Speed Trap:
S-L-O-W D-O-W-N

These are crazy times. There's a "disruption" a day.
Pant. Pant. Pant.
Speed is the key to personal success.
Speed is the key to enterprise success.
So, speed is the key to all good things????
Hold on . . .
On the following pages is a partial list of strategic
activities that underpin both personal and organizational
success and excellence, and cannot be accomplished in
a flash (or, for that matter, 100 flashes).

" Building/Maintaining
Relationships . . . takes (lots and
lots . . . and lots of!!!) time.

Recruiting Allies to Your Cause . . .
takes (lots of) time.

Building/Maintaining a
High-Performance Culture . . .
takes (lots and lots of) time.

Reading/Studying . . . takes (lots of) time.

Aggressive Listening . . . takes (lots of!!!) time.

MBWA/MBZA (Managing By Wandering/Zooming Around) . . . takes (lots of!!!) time. ▶

Hiring/Evaluating/Promoting . . .
takes (lots of!!!) time.

Extreme Humanism/
Emotionally Connective Design . . .
takes (lots and lots of) time.

Your Next (Excellent!) Email and
Yes, Text Message Too, . . . should
take (lots of) time.

The 'Last One Percent' of Any Task or Project . . . takes time.

E-X-C-E-L-L-E-N-C-E . . . takes (lots and lots of . . .) time.

'Bottom line': Rome was not built in a day, nor is Enterprise Excellence. Slow Down. 99

Tom Peters

Read!
Read!!
Read!!!

" In my whole life, I have known no wise people (over a broad subject matter area) who didn't read all the time—none. ZERO. You'd be amazed at how much Warren [Buffett] reads—and how much I read. "

Charles T. Munger, *Poor Charlie's Almanack: The Wit and Wisdom of Charles T. Munger* (vice chairman, Berkshire Hathaway/Buffett's #2)

50 Percent Unscheduled.

Avoid busy-ness, free up your time, stay focused on what really matters. Let me put it bluntly: every leader should routinely keep a substantial portion of his or her time—*I would say as much as 50 percent*—unscheduled. . . . Only when you have substantial 'slop' in your schedule—unscheduled time—will you have the space to reflect on what you are doing, learn from experience, and recover from your inevitable mistakes. 99

Dov Frohman, Intel superstar, *Leadership the Hard Way: Why Leadership Can't Be Taught and How You Can Learn It Anyway*

Self-Management/
Self-Perception:
Good Luck
with That . . .

"Being aware of yourself and how you affect everyone around you is what distinguishes a superior leader."

Cindy Miller, with Edie Seashore, in Sally Helgesen's "Masters of the Breakthrough Moment," *strategy+business*

" Leadership is . . . self-knowledge. . . .

Successful leaders are those who are conscious about their behavior and the impact it has on the people around them. . . .

They are willing to examine what behaviors of their own may be getting in the way. . . .

The toughest person you will ever lead is yourself. We can't effectively lead others unless we can lead ourselves. ,,

Betsy Myers, *Take the Lead: Motivate, Inspire, and Bring Out the Best in Yourself and Everyone Around You*

"There are three things extremely hard: steel, a diamond and to know one's self."

Ben Franklin

> " The biggest problem I shall ever face: the management of Dale Carnegie. "

Dale Carnegie

Positive:
30× More Powerful Than Negative

" Positive attention* . . . is thirty times more powerful than negative attention in creating high performance on a team. . . .

People don't need feedback. They need attention, and, moreover, attention to what they do the best. And they become more engaged and therefore more productive when we give it to them. "

Marcus Buckingham and Ashley Goodall, *Nine Lies About Work: A Freethinking Leader's Guide to the Real World*

---

*This seems to be so hard for so many to appreciate/learn!!! (Why?)

Kindness

" Three things in human life are important. The first is to be kind. The second is to be kind. And the third is to be kind. "

Henry James

" The deepest principle of human nature is the craving to be appreciated. "

William James

> **The [two] most powerful things in life are a kind word, a thoughtful gesture.**

Ken Langone, Home Depot cofounder, in "Langone's Legacy," *Leaders Magazine*

" **People who don't feel significant usually don't make significant contributions.** "

Mark Sanborn, customer service guru

> "Believe it or not, I have sent roughly 30,000 handwritten notes to employees [12 per work day] . . . over the last decade, from maintenance people to senior executives."

Douglas R. Conant, "Secrets of Positive Feedback," *Harvard Business Review* (former CEO, Campbell Soup)

K = R = P

**Kindness =
Repeat Business =
Profit**

Kindness Is Free

" [There is a] misconception that supportive interactions require more staff or more time and are therefore more costly.

Although labor costs are a substantial part of any hospital budget, more personalized interactions themselves add nothing to the budget. Listening to patients or answering their questions costs nothing. ▶

It could be argued that negative interactions—alienating patients, not advocating for their needs, limiting their sense of control—can be very costly. . . .

Angry, frustrated, or frightened patients may be combative, withdrawn, and less cooperative, requiring far more time than it would have taken to interact with them initially in a positive way. 🙸

Jo Anne L. Earp, Elizabeth A. French, Melissa B. Gilkey, *Patient Advocacy for Health Care Quality: Strategies for Achieving Patient-Centered Care*

Feel Good About Themselves

"Leadership is about how you make people feel—about you, about the project or work you're doing together, and especially about themselves."

Betsy Myers, *Take the Lead: Motivate, Inspire, and Bring Out the Best in Yourself and Everyone Around You*

> **When I left the dining room after sitting next to Gladstone, I thought he was the cleverest man in England. But when I sat next to Disraeli, I left feeling that I was the cleverest woman!**

Jennie Jerome, Winston Churchill's [American] mother, in *Disraeli*, by Christopher Hibbert

Apology Power

" I regard apologizing as the most magical, healing, restorative gesture human beings can make. It is the centerpiece of my work with executives who want to get better. "

Marshall Goldsmith, *What Got You Here Won't Get You There: How Successful People Become Even More Successful* (Marshall Goldsmith is arguably the #1 executive coach.)

You Must Care.

"The one piece of advice which I believe will contribute more to making you a better leader . . . provide you with greater happiness and . . . advance your career more than any other advice . . . and it doesn't call for a special personality [or] any certain chemistry . . . any one of you can do it and that advice is—you must care."

General Melvin Zais, address to senior officers, U.S. Army War College

FYI:
I Own
giveashitism.com

" Bedrock: All the leadership ideas herein are gibberish and an utter and absolute waste of time unless the leader or would-be leader really (really! really! no baloney, no ifs, ands, or buts!) gives-a-shit/cares about people.

Give-a-shit-ism = You must care = *Sine qua non.*

(Reminder: You want give-a-shit-ism? Hire for it! You want give-a-shit-ism? Promote for it!) "

Tom Peters

"Résumé Virtues"
vs.
"Eulogy Virtues"

I've been thinking about the difference between the résumé virtues and the eulogy virtues. The résumé virtues are the ones you list on your résumé, the skills that you bring to the job market and that contribute to external success. The eulogy virtues are deeper. They're the virtues that get talked about at your funeral, the ones that exist at the core of your being—whether you are kind, brave, honest or faithful; what kind of relationships you formed.

David Brooks, *The Road to Character*

He Took Good
Care of People

" In a way, the world is a great liar.

It shows you it worships and admires money, but at the end of the day it doesn't.

It says it adores fame and celebrity, but it doesn't, not really. The world admires, and wants to hold on to, and not lose, goodness.

It admires virtue. ▶

At the end it gives its greatest tributes to generosity, honesty, courage, mercy, talents well used, talents that, brought into the world, make it better.

That's what it really admires.

That's what we talk about in eulogies, because that's what's important.

We don't say, 'The thing about Joe was he was rich!'

We say, if we can . . .

'The thing about Joe was he took good care of people.' **99**

Peggy Noonan, "A Life's Lesson," on the life and legacy of journalist Tim Russert, *Wall Street Journal*

Grace in All We Do

For my 60th birthday, I wrote a book titled in full: *SIXTY*. Translation: Sixty things I really cared about. My closer, #60, was by definition a Big Deal. And it was but a single word: Grace. My commentary started with a quote from renowned designer Celeste Cooper:

> **My favorite word is grace—whether it's 'amazing grace,' 'saving grace,' 'grace under fire,' 'Grace Kelly.'**
>
> **How we live contributes to beauty—whether it's how we treat other people or how we treat the environment.**

Celeste Cooper, designer

My synonym finder, *Rodale's*, offers these analogies to grace: *elegance . . . charm . . . loveliness . . . kindness . . . benevolence . . . benefaction . . . compassion . . . beauty.* Grace in all we do. And the more rushed and harried, and potentially insensitive, we are, the more important grace is.

COVID-19 Leadership:
The Seven Commandments

" Be Kind.
Be Caring.
Be Patient.
Be Forgiving.
Be Present.
Be Positive.
Walk in the Other Person's Shoes. "

Tom Peters

Excellence
Is the
Next Five
Minutes

Excellence
Is the
Next Five
Minutes

Excellence is not an aspiration.

Excellence is not a mountain to climb.

Excellence is the ultimate short-term strategy.

Excellence is the next five minutes.

Excellence is your next 10-line email.

Excellence is the first three minutes of your next meeting.

Excellence is listening . . . really really ('fiercely,' 'aggressively') l-i-s-t-e-n-i-n-g.

Excellence is sending flowers to the hospital where your top customer's mom is having major surgery. ▶

Excellence is going out of your way to say 'Thank you' for something 'small.'

Excellence is pulling out all the stops at warp speed to respond to a 'minor' screw-up.

Excellence is adding a final touch to a final touch to a final touch.

Excellence is the next five minutes.

(Or-it-is-nothing-at-all.) ❞

Tom Peters

Excellence
Is a Moral Act

" Creating excellence is not a job.
Creating excellence is a moral act. "

Hugh MacLeod, gapingvoid

Afterword
Blinding Flashes
of the Obvious

I was exhausted. I had just finished a two-day (!) seminar for a YPO group. Two days was tough enough, but YPOers are demanding, always challenging and asking follow-up questions, etc. As a closer, I asked the attendees (from the stage) to give me some feedback. Well, it was good for my ego—they had liked it, liked it a lot.

Then a hand popped up from a guy I felt I'd really bonded with, Manny Garcia, one of Burger King's top franchisees, with a hundred or so locations in South Florida. Manny started, "I'm a busy guy, and two days is a lot of time to spend. And I didn't learn anything new."

"My heart sank" is much too mellow a description of what I felt. Then he continued, "This is the best seminar I've ever attended. It was a brilliant reminder of what matters, and we know it matters, but we don't do it in the heat of the battle. This program was a blinding flash of the obvious."

Well, this is my 20th—and last—book. I've repeated the key messages in every book: people (really) first, training to die for, only products and services that engender pride and make the world a little bit better, moral behavior is the "24/7" standard, leadership as an intimate activity (MBWA/Managing By Wandering Around), listening as leader skill #1, sustainability as our watchword, Excellence in all we do.

I'd call every idea in this list a "blinding flash of the obvious." And as we face a multitude of staggering local and global challenges, I'd say . . . start today—not tomorrow—now more than ever.

Tom Peters

by Nancye Green

Tom Peters was once summed up by Nancy Austin: "A human exclamation point who no longer needs his last name." That in itself wouldn't make him more than an interesting character if it were not for what fuels his passion and drove him, 40 years ago with Bob Waterman, to write one of the most important business books ever written: *In Search of Excellence*. His latest, *Excellence Now: Extreme Humanism*, has again been acknowledged as a business book, but also as one of the best books on humanism written in 2021. Perhaps this is an even greater honor. Because people—not a cliché, but truly, profoundly, people, and the honoring of their talents, hopes, dreams, desires—are what Tom tells us passionately drive any and all enterprise success, even the financial kind.

Born to a mother who valued hard work and drove Tom to personal excellence, he joined the Navy, went to Stanford, and got his MBA. He landed at McKinsey when serious people were still asking questions like how much money can we make, *and* what makes a great company? It might be said that his first book found him, when a research assignment handed to Bob and Tom found its most perfect place to grow. In the hearts and minds of these two profoundly thoughtful, soul-searching, brilliant thinkers, they defined a vision about the sacred purpose of human enterprise: a place where people go to spend their lives fulfilled and driven by a mission that serves community and society, as well as itself. There are tales to be told about where it went wrong—greed, "shareholder value", and the "me" generations, for example. Tom suffers for what we have lost and relishes the moments of victory.

This book is Tom's personal victory—reduced to its essence—and what he has been saying all along. Each book has represented a true partnership of words and their shaping. And when this last one was finally finished, as we were all missing the joy of the journey, it was not lost on me that this is exactly what Tom fights for every day he breathes. Collaboration, working toward a shared goal, the celebration of each part of the effort, a wonderful outcome to be proud of. It doesn't get more human than that.

Nancye Green

by Tom Peters

Nancye, cofounder of the consulting firm Donovan/Green, is widely and repeatedly recognized as one of the world's premier designers. A list of her awards and award-winning projects would literally fill half this book. She is a past president of both the American Institute of Graphic Arts, where she is also a recipient of its Gold Medal, and the International Design Conference in Aspen. She is currently chair of the Board of Directors of EcoHealth Alliance, on the Board of Trustees of The New School in New York City, and on the Hallmark Board of Directors. She was granted an honorary PhD from the Corcoran School of Art, was a member of the selection committee for the Presidential Awards for Design Excellence, and was selected to be in the TED register of the Most Creative People in America.

I asked Nancye to sum up her approach to design: "I love working with very smart people on big ideas that make a difference. I love to work, to figure things out, to take a figurative roomful of stuff—ideas, notions, points of view—and winnow, winnow, winnow until the simplest, most profound ideas emerge that anyone can understand. I will not lie, I love beautiful things. They make me happy, and I believe beauty and delight are a universal gateway drug to motivation. Hobbies? I love to read."

I have been a vocal champion of great design for a quarter of a century, but I didn't really know what that meant until I started working with Nancye. I gushingly acknowledged Nancye's contribution to my last book, *Excellence Now: Extreme Humanism* (she is responsible for the title as well as book design) and was prepared to gush again about her efforts with the book you are reading. And then I realized what I should have realized long before. Nancye was not the "designer" of this book; she was the coauthor, even the lead author. She took my words and wholly transformed them through her design—my "message" to readers is its look, feel, taste, touch, smell, and character. Hence, I am proud to introduce to you the coauthor of *Tom Peters' Compact Guide to Excellence*, Nancye Green.

The Excellence Now Campaign

"What you are doing right now will be the hallmark of your entire career."

Tom Peters

These tumultuous times of sociopolitical unrest and global pandemic demand deep engagement, human connection, and, yes, EXCELLENCE. In response, Tom Peters created the Excellence Now Campaign, tools intended to be his definitive lessons in excellence, lessons that focus on topics of surpassing importance, topics that are, in fact, more important now than ever. The tools include the two *Extreme Humanism* volumes and the *Excellence: Now More Than Ever* course series.

For more from Tom Peters, visit **TomPeters.com**

Excellence: Now More Than Ever
course series

This six-part course series offers a total of 99 Steps to Excellence, each followed by specific actions you can take NOW. That's 99 Steps and more than 99 action items. The goal of the course series is simple: to offer a helping hand implementing the strategies resulting from decades of Tom's research, whether it's for a 2-person accountancy, a 14-person training department, a 23-person nonprofit staff, or a division of a giant company.

To learn more about the *Excellence: Now More Than Ever* course series, scan the QR code.

Extreme Humanism volumes

Additional titles in the Excellence Now Campaign:

Excellence Now: Extreme Humanism

In this book Tom sets a high bar for leaders, especially important given the state of our very troubled and fast-moving world today. Why "Extreme Humanism"? Compassion is not only the right thing to do; it makes business sense. Tom will show how excellence in leadership is achieved by an obsessive focus on the growth of those you are leading. Winner of best leadership book of 2021 by *strategy+business* and awarded one of the best humanism books by BookAuthority.

Excellence Now: Extreme Humanism: The 43 Number Ones

A collection of 43 and actionable "true Number Ones," extracted from Tom's 43 years of leadership research. Each idea stands on its own and cannot be relegated to the middle or bottom of a list. Moreover, each of the 43 ideas supports the rest—and the complete set adds up to a tapestry of enterprise excellence.

Special Acknowledgments

This book, and the two that preceded it, would not have been possible without the contributions of a few very important people.

Shelley Dolley has been, in effect, Tom's "COO" for over 20 years. It is true that she is incredibly competent, but she is so much more. She doesn't "finish his sentences" . . . she starts them. On top of COO tasks, she is also a significant contributor to the content of his material. She "does it all" and does it brilliantly, thoughtfully, and at warp speed.

Stuardo Lopez is the enormously talented designer of this series of books. He is both gifted and blessed with intelligence, curiosity, and good humor, which has been tested mightily over the years, as we have become a team working together. With another gifted young designer, JayJ Walsh, we authors joyously threw them idea after idea, adding and subtracting, always thrilled that what came back was always at the high standard we set from the outset. There is not a doubt in our minds that these books—this book—would not be what they are without these two excellent designers.

And a big thanks to the instigator who pulled us all together, Julie Anixter, who is the epitome of Dream Big, and has been a guiding spirit of the Extreme Humanism project.